W9-AYX-198

THE STORY OF
CADMUS

Pamela Espeland
pictures by Reg Sandland

Carolrhoda Books, Inc., Minneapolis

Copyright © 1980 by CAROLRHODA BOOKS, INC.

All rights reserved. International copyright secured.
Manufactured in the United States of America

LIBRARY OF CONGRESS CATALOGING IN PUBLICATION DATA

Espeland, Pamela, 1951-
The story of Cadmus.

SUMMARY: Relates how Cadmus' quest for his lost sister
resulted in the founding of Thebes.

1. Cadmus (Greek mythology)—Juvenile literature. [1. Cadmus
(Greek mythology). 2. Mythology, Greek] I. Sandland, Reg.
II. Title.

PZ8.1.E83St   1980   291.1'3'0938 [E]   80-66795
ISBN 0-87614-128-9   lib. bdg.

   2   3   4   5   6   7   8   9   10   92   91   90   89   88   87   86   85   84   83   82

to David Porter, who loves what he teaches

ABOUT THIS STORY

Ancient Greece wasn't very big, but it was very important. All together, the Greek states made up an area about the size of Austria. From this tiny part of the world came many famous people and ideas.

The ancient Greek people were a lot like us. Over 2,000 years ago, their children played and went to school and watched the Olympic games. Grown-ups worked. They wrote plays and poems. They made laws. Their government was the beginning of Western democracy.

But the Greeks didn't know as much as we do about science. So they used myths to explain nature. When there was a storm at sea, they said, "Poseidon, the God of the Sea, must be angry!" When there was a good harvest, they said, "Demeter, the Goddess of the Earth, must be happy!" Not all myths explained nature, though. Some told about Greek history. And some were just good stories.

The Greek civilization lasted for a long time, but it could not last forever. Around 150 B.C., the Romans took it over. They also adopted the Greek gods and goddesses — they just changed their names to Roman names. (In this story the Greek names have been used.) Most Romans didn't really believe in the gods, but they did like to tell good stories. So they kept on telling the myths.

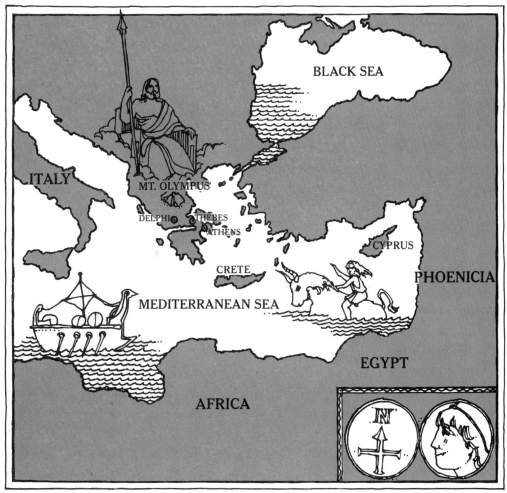

Cadmus's journey began in Phoenicia.

Many Greek and Roman writers liked the story of Cadmus and wrote it down. The Greeks thought it was a very important story. It told how their city of Thebes was built. It told how Cadmus was made the first king of the city.

Cadmus went on to have a big family. His family was called the House of Thebes. Many famous Greeks came from the House of Thebes. So the story of Cadmus was only the beginning.

When Cadmus woke up in the morning, the sun was shining brightly. A soft breeze blew in his window.

"What a perfect day to play in the meadow by the sea!" he said.

He ran to find his brothers and his little sister, Europa. Then they told their father, King Agenor, where they were going.

"Have fun," the king said, smiling. "And remember to take care of your sister!"

Cadmus and his brothers played tag in the tall grass. Europa gathered flowers. Soon the boys forgot all about her. They were having too much fun chasing each other and shouting. They left Europa all alone.

Europa sat down and waited for her brothers to come back. Suddenly she saw a big white bull. It was walking right toward her!

"Where did it come from?" she wondered aloud. "I'm sure it wasn't here just a minute ago!"

But there was an even bigger mystery about the bull. It wasn't really a bull at all. It was Zeus, the King of the Gods, playing a trick. He had looked down from his home on Mount Olympus and seen Europa sitting alone in the meadow.

"What a pretty little girl," he had thought. Then he had changed himself into a bull so he could sneak up on her.

At first Europa was a little bit afraid of the bull. But it was so pretty! And it didn't look at all mean. So she didn't run away. When the bull lay down in front of her, she climbed right up on its back.

But that wasn't very smart after all. The bull stood up and started running. It ran so fast Europa couldn't jump off. It ran through the meadow and right into the sea.

Cadmus looked around just in time to see what was happening.

"Wait!" he shouted. But it was too late. No one could save Europa now.

Cadmus and his brothers felt very sad. Europa was their only sister, and they loved her very much. They knew they should have watched her more closely. They also knew their father would be very angry with them. And he was.

"I told you to take care of your sister!" King Agenor shouted. Then he looked hard at Cadmus. "You're the oldest. You were in charge," the king said. "Now go out and find Europa. And don't come home without her!"

So Cadmus said good-bye to his mother and his brothers. Then he went down to the harbor. He found a ship and some sailors. He told them about Europa. And in the morning they all sailed away to look for her.

They went to town after town. In every town Cadmus asked the same question. "Has anyone seen a white bull with a little girl riding on its back?" But no one ever had.

Cadmus looked for Europa for many, many years. He got very tired, but he never gave up.

Then one day Cadmus decided he needed more help. In those days the best place to ask for help was in the town of Delphi. Apollo, the God of the Sun, had a temple there. It was a very special temple. Underneath it was a cave. And in the cave lived a spirit called the Oracle. Everyone knew that the Oracle could answer almost any question. It knew everything that was happening in the world.

So Cadmus went to Delphi to talk to the Oracle. The Oracle didn't always help people. But this time it did.

"Stop looking for Europa," the Oracle whispered. "Zeus took her away. She is safe. But you will never find her. Instead, look for a cow that is walking around all alone. Follow the cow. When it finally lies down, build a city on that spot."

Cadmus didn't want to stop looking for Europa. But he knew now that he would never find her. That same afternoon he saw a cow walking around all alone. So he called his men together. And they followed the cow.

They followed it up one hill and down another. Across one valley and through another. Cadmus had never seen a cow walk so far.

Finally the cow lay down in a grassy field. There were mountains all around it and a tall forest at one end.

"What a beautiful place!" said Cadmus. "I will build a city here."

Then Cadmus turned to his men.

"Go into the forest," he said. "Find a spring of fresh water. Bring some back. We will use it to thank the gods for leading us here."

So Cadmus's men went into the forest. It was very, very quiet. There was not even a wind to ruffle the leaves on the trees.

The men walked farther and farther. At last they heard a bubbling sound. Soon they found a spring of fresh water. It was flowing out of a dark cave.

The men started filling their pitchers. They talked and laughed together. They were glad their long journey was finally over. None of them heard the new sounds coming out of the cave. Hissing, slithering sounds.

Suddenly a huge dragon roared out of the cave! It was taller than the trees! Its scales glowed like fire! The last thing Cadmus's men ever saw was the dragon's mouth opening to bite them. It had three poisonous tongues! And three rows of gnashing, slashing teeth!

Meanwhile, Cadmus was waiting for his men to come back. "What is taking them so long?" he wondered. Finally he decided to go look for them.

When Cadmus came to the spring, he saw a horrible sight. All of his friends were dead! Then he heard the hissing, slithering sounds. He turned around just in time. The dragon was coming right at him!

Cadmus jumped away. He picked up a rock and threw it at the dragon. But it just bounced off. So he waited until the dragon opened its mouth. He saw the three poisonous tongues and the three rows of gnashing, slashing teeth. Then Cadmus threw his spear down the dragon's throat.

The dragon screamed! It lashed its huge tail back and forth! Cadmus felt its hot breath on his face. He was sure he was about to be killed. But then the dragon fell down. It was dead!

Cadmus walked back to the field. He was very sad. He missed his friends.

Suddenly he remembered that the Oracle had told him to build a city. But how could he do it all alone?

Then he heard a voice.

"Why are you standing there doing nothing?" it said.

Cadmus turned around. And there was Athena, the Goddess of Wisdom. He looked into her kind, gray eyes.

"Oh, Athena," he said. "What am I going to do? The Oracle told me to build a city here. But all my men are dead! And I can't build a city alone!"

Athena just smiled. "Listen to me, Cadmus," she said. "Go back to the dragon and pull out its teeth. Then plant them in the field."

This sounded strange to Cadmus. What good would it do to plant the dragon's teeth? But Athena was famous for helping people in trouble. Cadmus trusted her. So he went back into the forest. He pulled out the dragon's teeth. All three rows. Then he planted them in the field, one at a time. There were so many teeth that he lost count.

Finally Cadmus finished planting the teeth. He looked back at the field. He blinked. Were his eyes playing tricks on him? Or were there really spears growing out of the ground? Now brass helmets were pushing up like big, shiny beans! The dragon's teeth were growing into soldiers!

Soon the field was full of men! They looked very mean. For the second time that day, Cadmus was sure he was about to be killed. Then he heard Athena's soft voice again.

"Pick up a big stone," she said. "Then throw it at the soldiers. But don't let them see you do it!"

When Cadmus threw the stone, it hit some of the soldiers. They started shouting at one another.

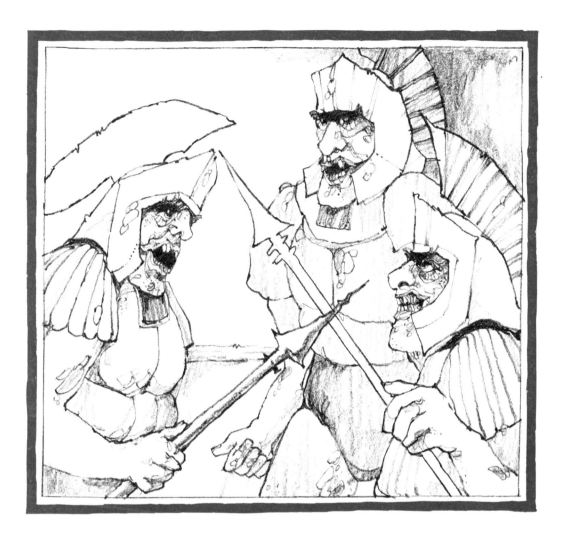

"Who threw that stone?"

"He threw it! I saw him!"

"Oh, no, I didn't! You did!"

The soldiers started fighting. It was a terrible battle. The air was filled with the sounds of clashing swords. When the battle was over, only the five strongest men were left alive. But they were hurt badly. So Cadmus helped them.

When they were well again, Cadmus told them the whole story. He told them about his little sister, Europa, and the bull. He told them about the Oracle. He told them how he had killed the dragon and planted its teeth.

"And now I have to build a city here," Cadmus said to the five soldiers. "Will you help me?"

The soldiers agreed to help. And that is how the city of Thebes was built. It was a beautiful city. People came from miles around to live there. They made Cadmus their king.

Thebes became a very large and important city. It lasted for a long, long time. Today there is a busy little town where Thebes used to be. And people still visit it to see the ruins of Cadmus's palace. The ruins are nearly 3,000 years old, but they still remind people of the boy who lost his sister and grew up to be a king.

PRONUNCIATION GUIDE

Agenor: uh-JEE-nor
Athena: uh-THEE-nuh
Cadmus: KAD-muss
Delphi: DELL-fie
Demeter: de-MEE-ter
Europa: you-ROE-puh
Olympus: oh-LIM-puss
Oracle: OR-uh-kull
Poseidon: poe-SIE-dun
Thebes: theebz
Zeus: zoose